I AM A SER>ANT

A FOUR-WEEK STUDENT DISCIPLESHIP JOURNAL

THIS BOOK BELONGS TO:

_____

Making Disciples...Developing Leaders

I Am a Servant
© 2015 by LeaderTreks. All rights reserved.

ISBN: 978-1-939031-25-9

No part of this publication may be reproduced, stored in a retrieval system, or transmitted in any form or by any means electronic or mechanical, including photocopy, recording, or any information storage and retrieval system now known or to be invented, without prior permission in writing from the publisher.

All Scripture quotations, unless otherwise indicated, are taken from the Holy Bible, New International Version®, NIV®. Copyright ©1973, 1978, 1984, 2011 by Biblica, Inc.™ Used by permission of Zondervan. All rights reserved worldwide. www.zondervan.com The "NIV" and "New International Version" are trademarks registered in the United States Patent and Trademark Office by Biblica, Inc.™

Published by LeaderTreks
25W560 Geneva Road, Suite 30
Carol Stream, IL 60188

www.leadertreks.com
877-502-0699

CONTENTS

Week One: What is a Servant?
Day One: Intro..4
Day One: Backwards 5
Day Two: Foundations 7
Day Three: Serve Like Christ 9
Day Four: Servants Never Retire 11
Day Five: Sacrificial Service 13
Day Six: Be A Mirror 15
Day Seven: Rest 17

Week Two: Who Do You Serve?
Day One: Intro..19
Day One: Unexpected Servants 21
Day Two: The Lost and the Least...23
Day Three: Guess Who? 25
Day Four: It's Not About Me 27
Day Five: Sacrificial Service 29
Day Six: Walking the Walk 31
Day Seven: Sabbath 33

Week Three: When Do You Serve?
Day One: Intro..36
Day One: A Chore 37
Day Two: Inconvenience..39
Day Three: Nothing to Show for It 41
Day Four: Our Best Laid Plans 43
Day Five: Sacrifice 45
Day Six: Invisible 47
Day Seven: Always Vigilant 49

Week Four: How Do We Serve?
Day One: Intro..52
Day One: At Arm's Length..53
Day Two: Prayer...55
Day Three: Serve With Words 57
Day Four: Service Undercover...59
Day Five: Here, There, Everywhere 61
Day Six: Into The World 63
Day Seven: Wrapping Up...65

Getting Started

In the early 17th century, pretty much everyone thought the earth was the center of the universe. It seemed obvious—the sun rose in the morning and set in the evening, and at night, the moon and stars seemed to spin across the sky. *Besides,* educated people thought, *we're pretty important, so it makes sense that everything else in the universe revolves around us.*

But Galileo Galilei had a different idea. After doing some complicated mathematical calculations, Galileo realized that the earth actually revolves around the sun. The earth wasn't the center of the universe at all! It just looked that way from our perspective. But when he tried to tell people about his discovery, the authorities weren't happy. They refused to believe the earth wasn't the center of the universe, so they locked Galileo under house arrest, where he eventually died.

Seems pretty crazy, right? How could people be so confused about something so obvious? The truth is, we're in a similar situation when it comes to service.

Most people think service is all about them. Even when they do things to help other people, it's really to help themselves. They pick up trash on the beach to get their picture in the paper. They serve in a soup kitchen to boost their college resume. They go on mission trips to brag about it on social media. It's as if the needs, the injustices, and the hurting people only exist to revolve around the real center of the universe: us.

This book was written to change that perspective. Like Galileo finding out that the earth actually revolves around the sun, you'll discover that service is actually centered on something much bigger than us. It revolves around Christ!

So prepare to shift your entire perspective on service. Are you willing to admit that you aren't the center of the universe? Are you ready to stop saying, "I serve when it's convenient," and start saying, "I am a servant, now and always"?

Let's Get Started.

HOW IT WORKS

This book includes four weeks of journal pages to challenge the way you understand service. Each week takes you through seven days of questions to get you thinking, bible studies to shift your perspective, and challenges to stretch you out of your comfort zone. Then, on the seventh day of the week, you'll get a break to recharge for the next section. It'll help you get into a rhythm of learning, growing, and putting that knowledge into action.

Throughout this journal, you'll also find the **Marks of a Disciple**. These are things that Christ-followers are committed to and have in common, especially when it comes to serving others.

Remember, you'll get out of this book what you put into it. The challenges you'll encounter won't always be easy—they're designed to stretch you! Take a risk and do your best to engage each day with energy and passion. When we make ourselves available to God, he'll transform us and use us in ways that will blow our minds!

Week One
WHAT IS A SERVANT?

DAY ONE
INTRO

If you earned your medical degree, worked for years as an intern and a resident, and started working at a hospital, you wouldn't think of yourself as someone who, treats patients from time to time. You're a doctor! Even when you're on vacation, if you see someone collapse in the street or get sick on a plane, you have an obligation to help out. Just because you aren't in the office doesn't mean you aren't still in doctor-mode.

Service is the same. We go on mission trips and service projects hoping to do some good, but the minute we get home, we feel like we're off the clock. But people's needs don't just stop after a week (or day, or month!) of service. That's why true service, the kind that Jesus showed us, requires us to change our thinking. It means we don't think of service as a once-in-a-while kind of thing. Instead, we start seeing ourselves as servants—always on the lookout for those who need our help.

Backwards

Our culture values service. Pretty much everyone believes that good service should be rewarded and bad service should be punished. The size of a tip depends on the quality of service. We feel like we deserve to be served—not just in restaurants, but everywhere. Imagine how much of your day would be different without people serving you. You'd have to face tests completely unprepared, you'd have to crawl through mounds of trash and step over vomit in the halls, and you'd probably go hungry when lunch rolled around.

Just think about how frustrating it is when the Internet goes out and no one can fix it until the next day. When people aren't serving us, we feel like our world has been thrown off kilter. By assuming that we deserve to be waited on, we have developed a distorted understanding of what service is.

Jesus was born over 2,000 years ago, but his culture wasn't that different from our world. Just like us, many people felt like they deserved to be served. In Matthew 20:28 Jesus says, *"The Son of Man did not come to be served, but to serve, and to give his life as a ransom for many."*
Jesus came to set the record straight. He knew that people had the whole concept of service backwards. And that's the same problem we have today.

This week we will approach the idea of service from God's perspective to discover the many ways we have it backwards.

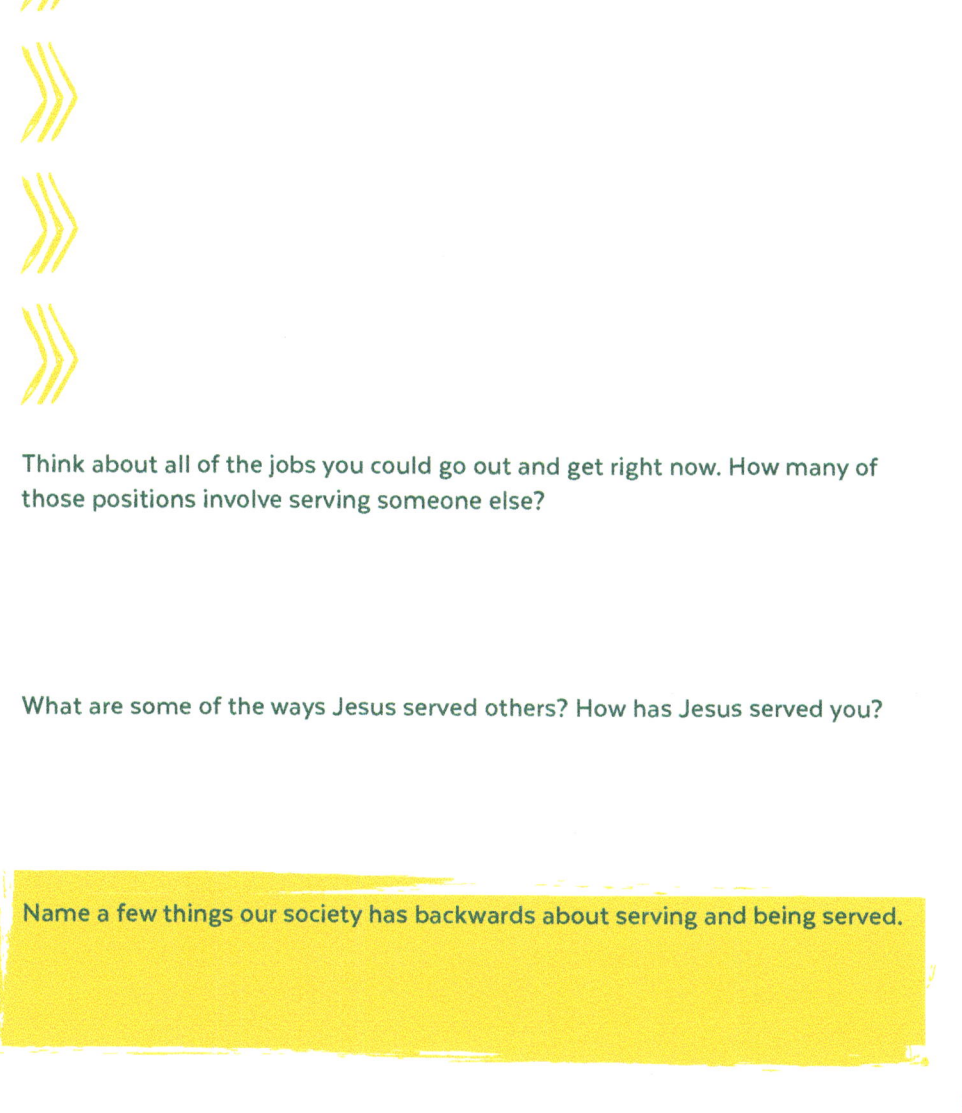

When was the last time someone served you at a restaurant? At school? At home? Somewhere else? Make a list of 20.

》》

》》

》》

》》

Think about all of the jobs you could go out and get right now. How many of those positions involve serving someone else?

What are some of the ways Jesus served others? How has Jesus served you?

Name a few things our society has backwards about serving and being served.

DAY TWO
FOUNDATIONS

It is easy to get confused about service when we see it as something we do instead of something we are. Our lives are changed when we enter a relationship with Christ. Are you willing to let Jesus transform you from the inside out so that works of service flow out of your new identity?

In the Old Testament, we see many countries and people who worshiped idols. They made statues out of stone and wood and believed those idols would give them riches, status, and health. By worshipping these objects, they often ended up serving themselves. After all, it's not like the stone statues were telling them what to do!

When we follow Christ, we take on a new identity. We become servants. But unlike the idol worshipers, we are called to serve other people, not ourselves. That doesn't happen all at once. Sometimes we continue serving objects (and, in turn, ourselves). Think about the amount of time you devote to things like TV shows, video games, social media, popularity, or sports. Some of those are good things, but if we spend too much time "worshiping" them, they can distract us from the new life Jesus wants us to live.

We were made to serve. If we don't serve God and the people he loves, then we will serve other things. In order to understand true service, we must first be transformed into servants by following Jesus.

Take a look at 2 Corinthians 5:16-21 using the 5P Bible study method. Here, Paul explains how Jesus transforms us into new creations, and then calls us to live out that transformation.

PURPOSE

Why do you think the author wrote this? Why is it important enough to be in the Bible? In a sentence or two, write what you think the overall theme or topic is.

PRIMARY VERSE

Which verse seems to contain the most important thought in the passage? Which one stands out most to you? Write out the verse completely and the corresponding reference.

PROMISES

Make a list of any promises you find. Sometimes you need to infer promises from a passage. For example, John 3:16 does not come right out and promise you heaven. But it implies a promise: "If you believe, you will have eternal life."

PROBLEMS

If you find anything you don't understand—even if it's just a word—write it down as a question. Then ask someone for the answer or look it up yourself. One way to know if you have any problems is to ask yourself, "Is there anything in this passage that I could not explain to a friend?"

PRACTICAL APPLICATION

Think about what the passage means to you. What action should you take? What do you need to change or work on so that what you have read is real in your life? Be specific—your application should tell who, what, and when.

DAY THREE
SERVE LIKE CHRIST

When we love God with everything in us, we follow his commands. We begin to love the things and the people he loves. We see the immense value of those God created in his image—and that includes everyone.

As you probably know, loving others can be difficult. Before we see God's image in people, we see their flaws, quirks, and differences. Have you ever met someone at school with opposite views as you? You probably have an unwritten list of people you avoid at school or block on social media because they drive you nuts.

Yet that's exactly who Jesus came into the world to love. People bothered Jesus constantly, and he got exasperated with them from time to time (Matt. 17:17). The people he came to save rejected him, denied him, and hung him on a cross. But even after all of that, he died to save them from their sins. We tend to see others as annoying or lowly and ourselves as charitable when we reach out to help them. But the truth is, we've all rejected Jesus—yet he still loves us and died to serve us.

What would happen if you stepped out in obedience to God and served that person you don't like? What if you chose to treat them well, open the door for them, encourage them, or invite them to your house? Maybe by serving them the way Christ served others (and you), you will begin to see others the way Christ sees them.

TAKE THIS CHALLENGE:

Do one of the following to stretch yourself this week. Serve people you wouldn't normally serve. Serve in places you wouldn't normally go. Then write about that experience in the space provided.

 Go out of your way to compliment or encourage someone on social media whom you wouldn't normally connect with.

 Call someone you don't regularly talk to from your youth group and ask how you can pray for them.

 Go through your closet and give away your favorite outfit to someone who needs it more than you.

 Pick a teacher you aren't close to. Ask what their favorite beverage is, then buy it for them.

DAY FOUR
SERVANTS NEVER RETIRE

The comforting thing about only serving when we feel like it is that we know there's a finish line. If things get difficult and we just want to quit, we can tell ourselves, *Don't worry; you only have to serve for three more days!* And if things get really tough, we find a way out for ourselves—an eject button to push when we're tired of serving.

But living with a servant identity is different. All-the-time servants don't look for a way out when things get tough. They don't count down the hours until they "don't have to serve anymore." Since their servant lifestyle never ends, they learn to appreciate service in a way "part-time" servants never will. They work until the job is done, because service is about helping other people as much as possible, not about making ouselves feel good. And it connects them to Jesus in a unique way because he is our primary example—a servant who never stopped serving, even when it led to his death.

Check out this quote from pastor Rick Warren. Then answer the following questions to dig deeper into what he's talking about.

> "FAITHFUL SERVANTS NEVER RETIRE. THEY SERVE FAITHFULLY AS LONG AS THEY'RE ALIVE. YOU CAN RETIRE FROM YOUR CAREER, BUT YOU WILL NEVER RETIRE FROM SERVING GOD."
>
> –Rick Warren, "Servants Finish Their Tasks"

Do you ever get tired of serving others?

Describe a time when you were helping someone out but just wanted to give up and go home.

Why do you think pastor Rick Warren says, *"Faithful servants never retire"*?

What strategies might help you stick with a service project you really want to quit?

Disciples of Christ NEVER STOP serving. (Romans 12:11)

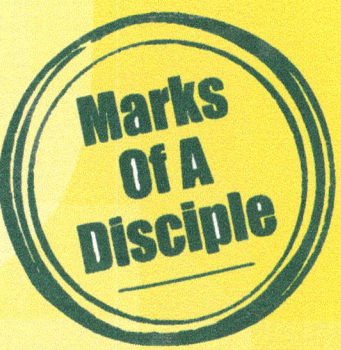

DAY FIVE
SACRIFICIAL SERVICE

Serving others usually requires some form of sacrifice. When we do something for someone else, we give up our time, money, or comfort. Becoming a servant means putting others' needs above our own desires.

The ultimate example of serving is when Jesus died for our sins. It was the most valuable thing anyone has ever done for us, but it required a huge sacrifice. Jesus gave up his immediate desire for safety and security because he loved us and knew what we needed more than we did.

Today you'll read about Jesus washing his disciples' feet in John 13. Why do you think he did that? And why did he think it was so important, that he would spend part of his last few hours with them, washing their feet? Weren't there other, more important things to do with time running out? He was giving them an example to follow because he knew he would be leaving them soon. It was an act of sacrificial service—something a servant would normally do. Jesus served his followers because he loved them, but also because he wanted them to become more like him. When we serve one another based on his example, we'll start to look more and more like him.

Jesus set the example for how to serve God and others. Use the OPA method to study John 13:1-9. Discover what serving others looked like to him.

OBSERVATION

Compile all the facts found in these passages. Make 20-30 observations about what you read.

PRINCIPLES

Draw a few principles from the observations you made. What is God trying to teach you in this passage?

APPLICATION

How will you apply these principles to your life? Be specific—a good application will tell who, what, and when.

DAY SIX
BE A MIRROR

Imagine that you began to live out Jesus' mission to serve others. You prayed for an opportunity to serve others, and when that opportunity came up, you took it. You started cleaning up for others at lunch every day without being asked. You didn't care if anyone noticed. You gave up five to ten minutes of time hanging out with friends each day to serve your classmates and teachers. No one ever asked or mentioned anything to you. You simply served in a small way, expecting nothing in return.

Then at the end of your senior year, a student signed your yearbook and shared the impact that your small act of service had on them. They wrote that they noticed you picking up after others each day and they admired you for it. They shared that they could sense God's love and faithfulness through your faithful work.

Then another student wrote something similar. Then another. Eventually your entire yearbook was filled with the appreciation of other students and teachers. You discovered that many students noticed what you'd done and were drawn to God through the small example you set.

Would that actually happen if you did this act of service? Probably not. Yet wouldn't it be worth it if just one person saw Jesus in your actions? You have the potential to make a tremendous impact on those around you. God calls each of us to be a mirror that reflects him to the rest of the world. One part of that is through regular, humble service. How can you reflect Jesus and influence the people in your life?

Start by taking the following challenge:

An Open Hand

Live the next two days with an "open hand." Whenever someone asks you for something, give it to them immediately. When someone asks you to do something, just do it, no questions asked (obviously, only if it's in the bounds of safety and morality). As you live these days open handed, think about the things you'd normally keep for yourself. Take note of the things you would usually say no to automatically. Once the two days are over, answer these questions:

Were you surprised by the number of times you gave away or did something you wouldn't have if you weren't living out the "open hand" challenge? Why or why not?

What were some of the things you had to give away? What were some of the things you had to do?

How did you feel after the two days were up? Was it difficult? Would you choose to keep living this way for a week?

DAY SEVEN
REST

Just because you're an all-the-time servant doesn't mean you should never take a break. When God created the world, he ended his work by resting on the seventh day. Do you think the almighty God of the universe actually needed a nap? Of course not! He was setting an example for us.

There's a difference between taking a short break to recharge, and looking for excuses to stop serving entirely. So go ahead and take today off! Use this break to recharge your batteries and refresh your mind. Then come back tomorrow, ready to dig into service again!

If you've finished the "Open Hand" challenge from yesterday, spend some time answering the questions that followed it.

"By the seventh day God had finished the work he had been doing; so on the seventh day he rested from all his work."
-Genesis 2:2

Week Two
WHO DO YOU SERVE?

DAY ONE
INTRO

When we're asked the question, Who are we supposed to serve?, it's tempting to give an easy answer: everyone! And while there's truth to that, there's another answer that will be more helpful in guiding our actions. First and foremost, we should seek to serve God. He's the only one worthy of our daily service and worship.

Let's look at that a little closer. When we read through the Bible, we discover that God loves the people he created more than we can ever imagine. In fact, he loves people most of us would never imagine loving on our own: the least, the lost, and our enemies. So when we choose to serve God, we also choose to serve the people he loves. Anyone can serve people they like. Anyone can serve people who will turn around and serve them back. ("I scratched your back, so you scratch mine.") But it takes a deep commitment to Christ to drive us into unfamiliar territory—serving the least, the lost, and our enemies because we want to love the people God loves.

UNEXPECTED SERVANTS

Close your eyes. Think for a moment about the last time you went out to eat. Perhaps it was to your favorite local burger joint, maybe for burritos, or wheatgrass smoothies, or extra-spicy Pad Thai. (Getting hungry yet?)

What was the name of the person who served you your meal? Did you notice the color of their eyes? Did they seem happy, or just going through the motions of their job? If you're like most people in our culture, you probably didn't notice—you figured they were just there to serve. As long as they did their job, you didn't pay much attention.

Maybe you've been that person, working a job that everyone takes for granted. No one sees you as someone who really matters. Have you felt unappreciated when you've served someone else? Unseen?

As you discovered last week, who-serves-whom can be a mixed-up concept for us. On the one hand, we depend on other people for basic needs like sanitation, food, heating, safety, and housing more than at any other time in human history. But we hardly ever see the people whose service makes such a difference in our lives. If we're honest with ourselves, we have to admit that we carry some mixed-up ideas about who we serve as Christ-followers.

When our actions flow out of our identities as followers of Christ, service becomes something . . . unexpected.

>> **It's not something the weak do for the powerful.**
>> **It's not something the poor do for the rich.**
>> **It's not something the awkward do for the popular.**
>> **It's not something we do for those who "deserve" it.**
>> **It's not something we do for those who can reward us.**
>> **It's not something we do for those who show their gratitude.**

Christ-like service is unexpected, just like Jesus' ministry on earth. Service is surprising! It turns the world upside down through simple, selfless acts. God wants to use it to transform our hearts and our communities. For who? For the whole world!

What are some of the things that make service difficult?

Who do you know that serves selflessly? What motivates them?

Who is the hardest person (or type of person) for you to serve? Why?

How did Jesus serve people unexpectedly? Write down one specific example.

DAY TWO
THE LOST AND THE LEAST

Have you ever seen the reality show *Undercover Boss*? Leading executives of huge corporations leave their posh offices to spend time doing hands-on work with the employees at the bottom of the business ladder. When these employees discover that their new co-worker actually runs the company, their reactions are priceless. Some, who have treated the "new guy" with compassion and understanding, are overjoyed that their hard work has been noticed. Others, who haven't been so kind, are terrified that someone they thought had no power has all the power.

That picture, of the boss becoming a burger-flipper, is a lot like how Jesus, who is God, took on our human nature to be a servant to the world. His example of humility and sacrifice defines true service.

It also defines the long-term way we are to serve and behave in God's kingdom. Just like Jesus served the lost and the least, so are we to serve. The people who are "worthless" in the eyes of the world are lifted up in God's kingdom. Those least able to give thanks or a reward are the ones we are most called to live for.

Yesterday, you thought through the unexpected recipients of Christian service. God surprises us by turning our culture's ideas about who-serves-whom upside down. But that's hard! It demands that you be seen with those you'd rather not be seen with, to spend time doing things that you'd probably rather not do, and maybe even to suffer in solidarity with the unpopular, the rejected, the forgotten. We are called to serve everyone, and whether or not we want to admit it, that includes the poor, the lost, and the least.

What that means is beautiful. And terrifying.

Today, we'll study Jesus' teaching in Matthew 23:1-12.
Study the passage using the OPA method.

OBSERVATION

Compile all the facts found in these passages. Make 20 to 30 observations about what you read.

PRINCIPLES

Draw a few principles from the observations you made. What is God trying to teach you in this passage?

APPLICATION

*How will you apply these principles to your life?
Be specific—a good application will tell who, what, and when.*

DAY THREE
GUESS WHO?

Yesterday, we studied the way Jesus' teaching changes how we think about unexpected service. To be great in God's kingdom, we transform into servants, seeking out the poor, the lost, and the least to show God's love.

Now it's time to get creative. In this challenge, you'll read the categories of people in need of unexpected service. Write the name of someone you can serve in that category. Then write your first idea for how to serve that person in the LEFT column. Be specific! If you need help thinking of something, check out the column on the RIGHT for bonus ideas on unexpected service.

"You have not lived today until you have done something for someone who can never repay you."
-John Bunyan, Pilgrim's Progress

Someone in Poverty–Name:

Idea for Service:

Think beyond giving this person money or something valuable. How can you make them feel seen, noticed, important? Sometimes service is as simple as showing someone that they matter to you.

Someone Sick–Name:

Idea for Service:

For someone with a chronic illness, is there anything you can do regularly that they can look forward to? For someone with a short-term sickness, what can you do to help ease their daily routine as they recover?

An Unbeliever–Name:

Idea for Service:

Serving this person starts by showing them that you genuinely love and respect them—while always being ready to share Christ's love and truth.

Someone Unpopular–Name:

Idea for Service:

What can you do to show this person love and acceptance? Are you willing to include them in an event or activity you've been looking forward to?

An Enemy–Name:

Idea for Service

Here's where unexpected service gets real. Consider asking a pastor or mentor for ideas on loving this person. Are you willing to serve even if they aren't willing to receive it?

DAY FOUR
IT'S NOT AOUT ME

Most of us are eager to help out our friends. We might even be okay with serving strangers, as long as it gives us a warm, fuzzy feeling afterward. But what about the jerk? What about the person who needs your help, but doesn't want it? What about the people who have gone out of their way to make your life miserable?

Many people live as if service is about balancing a scale—if someone helps me out, I'm obligated to help them. But that kind of service is built on pride, not love. It cuts people who aren't able to serve others out of the loop.

As anyone who watched children's television between 1968 and 2001 knows, one person who really understood what it meant to serve people was Fred Rogers of *Mister Rogers' Neighborhood*. Think about this quote from Mister Rogers by answering the following questions.

> "I hope you're proud of yourself for the times you've said 'yes,' when all it meant was extra work for you and was seemingly helpful only to someone else."
>
> –Fred Rogers,
> *The World According to Mister Rogers: Important Things to Remember*

Have you ever said "yes" to a selfless service opportunity? If so, how did that make you feel?

Why can't we expect people to reward us every time we serve them?

What roadblocks are keeping you from serving annoying, frustrating, and just plain mean people?

Disciples of Christ serve without expecting REWARDS. (Luke 6:33)

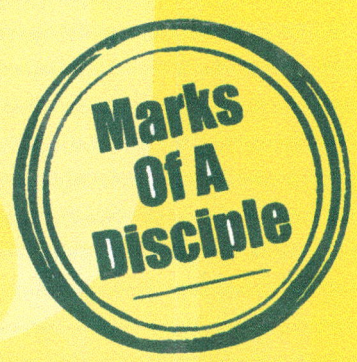

DAY FIVE
SACRIFICIAL SERVICE

Have you ever seen the movie Napoleon Dynamite? There's a classic scene where the (very) awkward main character invites a popular girl from school to a dance. Out of pity for Napoleon, the girl's mom makes her go with him. But what's the first thing that happens when they get to the event? She ditches him to join her friends. You see, even though she was going through the motions of unexpected service, her heart wasn't in the right place. Once the source of her motivation (her mom's glare) was gone, so was she. Napoleon was left in a worse situation than if he hadn't gone with her at all.

As Christ-followers, when we serve half-heartedly or for the wrong reasons, it can make things worse. It can take away dignity, make people feel used, and feed our pride-which only gets in the way of our relationship with Jesus. Instead, serve because you want to follow Christ and become like him. Serve because God places an incredible value on all people, even (maybe especially) the people that the world would like to ignore.

So far we've seen the true nature of unexpected service, learned about the recipients of that service (the poor, the lost, and the least), and brainstormed who in our lives could use a taste of God's unexpected service through us. Now let's add a little bit more: why the poor, the lost, and the least are so valuable in God's kingdom.

Study James 2:2-7 using the SPECK method. While you're reading, consider why the lost and least matter so much to God.

INS TO AVOID

Make a list of any sins—wrong actions, attitudes, or thoughts—mentioned in the passage. These are the things to avoid in your life.

ROMISES TO CLAIM

Make a list of the promises in this passage. Promises give us confidence when we doubt God or face difficult times. So take them to heart and believe what they say.

XAMPLES TO FOLLOW

What examples do you find in the passage? Is there a right way of thinking or acting described in the passage that you should take as an example for your life? Write it down.

OMMANDS TO OBEY

Write out all the commands you find. If a passage encourages you to take a certain action, take it as a command and write it down.

NOWLEDGE OF GOD TO APPLY

What does the passage tell you about God that you can apply to your daily life? God's character shines throughout the Bible as an example for us.

DAY SIX
WALKING THE WALK

Today caps off your week of thinking about who to serve. It's about to get real.

Go back and look at the list you made on Day 3. You brainstormed five names and came up with creative ways to bring unexpected service to each of them. Copy those names and your service ideas here (we'll talk about the "Obstacle" and "Solution" columns in a minute):

Name	Idea for Service	Obstacle	Solution

With this list, you have zeroed in on some important people you can be an unexpected servant to. You've gotten specific about one way you can serve them. But let's be realistic—good intentions are easy. Staying accountable to those intentions . . . well, that's harder.

We're going to do two things to cement your strategy to live out God's plan for service in your life.

FIRST
, think about what obstacle stands in your way for serving each of these people. Does one of them live far away? The obstacle might be the distance and time to get to them. Are you (if you're honest) not that eager to reach out to an enemy—someone who's hurt you? That's natural, but it's still an obstacle (perhaps fear or resentment). You get the point. Write the honest, specific obstacles that you can think of in the appropriate column.

SECOND
(you saw this coming), write your best idea for a realistic, specific solution to the obstacle. Who can you partner with? How can you make time? If a little money's needed for an idea, where will that come from? This is your chance to plan.

Is your grid all filled out? What do you think—is this what realistic service looks like for you, right here, right now? How will you make sure these ideas actually happen? How will life be different (for you and for others) if you serve in these ways?

Now, spend a few minutes in quiet thought and prayer. Give this list to God, and listen for his voice as you prepare to live it out. Turn off your phone, step away from your computer, go somewhere quiet, and just have a chat with God.

DAY SEVEN
SABBATH

Have you heard the word *Sabbath* before? It's something God came up with. Remember last week when we talked about God resting on the seventh day of creation? Well he told his followers to do the same thing. One day out of every week, God's people are commanded to take a break from work.

But Sabbath isn't the same thing as laziness. God calls the Sabbath a day dedicated "to the Lord your God." So take this day as a Sabbath from this journal—don't worry about doing any challenges or thinking through any journal responses. Instead, spend that time appreciating your relationship with God. Like any relationship, your relationship with God requires quality time and communication. That's exactly what a Sabbath day is for.

> "The highest form of worship is the worship of unselfish Christian service. The greatest form of praise is the sound of consecrated feet seeking out the lost and helpless."
>
> - Billy Graham

"Remember the Sabbath day by keeping it holy. Six days you shall labor and do all your work, but the seventh day is a sabbath to the Lord your God."

Exodus 20:8-10a

Week Three
WHEN DO YOU SERVE?

DAY ONE
INTRO

At this point in your life, your schedule probably works like a well-oiled machine. Get up. Eat breakfast. Go to morning classes. Eat lunch. Go to afternoon classes. Go to practice. Eat dinner. Do homework. Chat with friends. Go to bed. Repeat.

But every once in a while, something happens—even a tiny glitch—that throws everything out of whack. Suppose you sleep through your alarm in the morning. You miss breakfast because you're in a rush. You're late to your first class. You make up for breakfast by eating more for lunch. Now, you're sleepy during your afternoon classes. You're late for practice because you forgot your shoes in your morning rush, so now you're running laps. Meanwhile, your ride home is mad because he's stuck waiting for you to finish. No wonder we hate when things don't go as planned.

But being a servant requires flexibility. If you're always in servant-mode, you can't be surprised when your busy schedule doesn't go as planned. Service requires sacrifice, and sometimes that means giving up our time. How can we offer our time as a gift to God and people in need? You'll find out this week.

A CHORE

Imagine your job is to recruit high school students to serve for free. How would you do it?

You could focus on how it will help them. Show them the pro athlete who gains fame and endorsement money because he gives to charity. Focus on the latest Hollywood stars visiting Africa to hug orphans and take photo ops. Remind them that community service gives an edge on college applications and scholarship forms. Describe the warm feeling you get when you help someone who needs it.

But none of that compares with God's perspective on serving. Service gives us the opportunity to stand with Jesus and aid those who matter most to him. **When you serve, you're partnering with the creator of the entire universe to care for the things he cares about.** It's one of the reasons he created you in the first place. No college scholarship or community service award can compete with that!

Thankfully we don't have to cross the world to partner with God in service. Mission trips, service projects, feeding the hungry, and housing the homeless are all extremely close to God's heart. But so are the everyday things that no one would ever advertise—babysitting the neighbors' kid, noticing the new student at school, or doing dishes after dinner so your parents can rest. Service isn't just a project; it's who we are. When we serve, we're learning to enjoy the things Jesus enjoys, to be like him. It's how we reflect the heart of God to a hurting world. And it can happen all the time, wherever we go.

This week we're going to think about some of the best times and opportunities to serve, in big ways and in everyday life.

What was the most meaningful service experience you've ever been a part of? Was it planned or unplanned?

Think of a time when you spontaneously served someone. How was that different from service opportunities that are planned in advance?

Think back to the question at the top of this day: how would you recruit fellow students to serve for free?

What is your favorite part of serving? Why do you like it? What's your least favorite part? Why?

DAY TWO
INCONVENIENCE

Imagine that your cousin just died. He was one of your best friends. His friends just told you that he was executed in jail even though he didn't do anything wrong. The picture haunts you. He didn't deserve to die. You're reeling, emotionally ambushed, and you feel absolutely alone. You feel a horrible weight in the pit of your stomach. No one else understands—not really. The grief is simply exhausting.

What do you want most in that moment? Crowds of people? Probably not. You just want to get away, to be alone, to have a few moments to think, to cry, to process, and to heal.

But opportunities to serve don't always happen on our schedule. We're rushing out the door to a friend's house when we see our elderly neighbor trying to shovel their driveway. We're already slammed with homework when a friend needs someone to listen to their problems. And your mom or dad always ask for help around the house right when you're about to hang out with friends. People need us to serve them at the most inconvenient times.

Jesus finds himself in this exact situation in Matthew 14:6-21. As you read this passage, try to put yourself in Jesus' shoes.

Choose one of the study methods we've used during the last two weeks: 5P (page 8), OPA (page 24), or SPECK (page 30) and imagine what Jesus is experiencing.

DAY THREE

NOTHING TO SHOW FOR IT

Rob will never forget the time he decided to serve another high school student named Seth. Rob doesn't even remember Seth's last name, but he remembers how Seth tested his commitment to service. There's probably someone like Seth in your world, too. He was the guy everyone loved to hate. But for some reason, Seth liked to talk to Rob.

It was Rob's senior year of high school, and he was a brand-new student in a school of 2,100 people. His family had moved just two weeks before school started, so he wasn't exactly socially established. Neither Rob nor Seth had any friends. In Rob's case, it was because he was new. In Seth's case, well . . . the list was long. It included things like hygiene problems, weird clothes, and a reputation for other disgusting habits.

Rob, in his old, silver Honda Accord, would often pass Seth on the way home from school. Seth walked along the side of the road. Each time, a war waged in Rob's heart: *Should I stop and offer him a ride? Yeah, I probably should—it's the right thing to do. But what if someone sees me? What if they think I like him? What if they think I'm like him?*

One day, Rob finally took a deep breath and stopped to pick him up. He waited for Seth to say, "Thank you." Instead, Seth just made fun of Rob's car, and then sat silently all the way to his house.

Sometimes serving others is hard. Sometimes it's the last thing we want to do. Sometimes it comes with no reward, no good feelings, no happiness or joy. It's just difficult, and we don't want to do it.

Seth didn't come to know Jesus from the time Rob reached out to give him a ride. Rob and Seth didn't become close friends. But one thing is true: God loves Seth, and God calls you to serve people like him—even when there's nothing to show for it.

Be honest—would you help out someone like Seth if you knew you'd have nothing to show for it afterward?

What about this story makes you nervous or frustrated? Does anything about it encourage you?

Yesterday we looked at Jesus serving a crowd when he didn't want to. Why do you think Jesus chose to serve that crowd?

Think of a time someone served you when you really needed it. How did that make a difference in your life?

Why do you think we tend to serve only when there's some sort of reward (even if that reward is feeling good about ourselves)?

DAY FOUR
OUR BEST LAID PLANS

Have you ever planned something—a party or a night out with friends—that completely fell apart? Maybe you planned to spend the day outside, but rain kept you indoors. Perhaps you wanted to eat at your favorite restaurant, but it was super crowded and you didn't have reservations. All the energy you put into planning, all the anticipation you built up in your mind—all for nothing.

We can respond to these situations in two ways. First, we can give in to the frustration and sulk. Our day is ruined, and we throw up our hands in defeat. Or, second, we can embrace those interruptions. Think about your favorite book, TV show, or movie—if everything happened the way the main characters wanted it to, would you still enjoy the story? Of course not! The interruptions and complications make the story interesting. Where our plans end, adventure begins.

C.S. Lewis understood what it felt like to have his plans interrupted. Even though he had been a strong atheist for most of his life, Lewis's plans were interrupted by his friendship with J.R.R. Tolkien and the writings of G.K. Chesterton. Through these influences, Lewis became a follower of Jesus, "kicking, struggling, resentful, and darting his eyes in every direction for a chance to escape." But what felt like an interruption to his plans became a moment that defined his work until the day he died. Think about this quote by C.S. Lewis by answering the following questions.

"The great thing, if one can, is to stop regarding all the unpleasant things as interruptions of one's 'own,' or 'real' life. The truth is of course that what one calls the interruptions are precisely one's real life—the life God is sending one day by day."

–C.S. Lewis, from a 1943 letter included in *Yours, Jack: Spiritual Direction from C.S. Lewis*

Why do interruptions frustrate us so much?

Have you ever felt like an interruption when you needed something from someone else? What made you feel that way?

What is one thing you can do to stop seeing frustrating people as interruptions and start seeing them as an important part of your life?

Disciples of Christ see people as blessings, not INTERRUPTIONS. (Philippians 2:3)

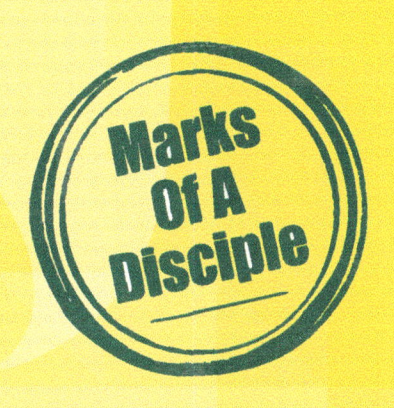

Marks Of A Disciple

DAY FIVE
SACRIFICE

We've all been there—that moment when someone asks us to serve, and it's the last thing we want to do in the world. You're getting ready in the morning and your older sister demands extra time in the bathroom. Or after school, your younger brother begs you to drive him to soccer practice. At moments like these, serving is not glamorous or fun.

Let's be honest: service is hard. More often than not, we wouldn't choose to trade our free time to help other people. That's why, to become true servants, we need our hearts to change. That happens when we grow as disciples of Jesus.

Have you ever thought about what it cost Jesus to come to earth? Imagine the culture shock. Jesus left heaven to come here! This was the greatest missionary journey of all time— from a heavenly throne to an animal food trough. Eventually Jesus was convicted and executed for claiming to be exactly who he was: God. This was no heroic death. It was torturous and painful. He made all of these sacrifices so we could live in eternal relationship with him. Now that's service.

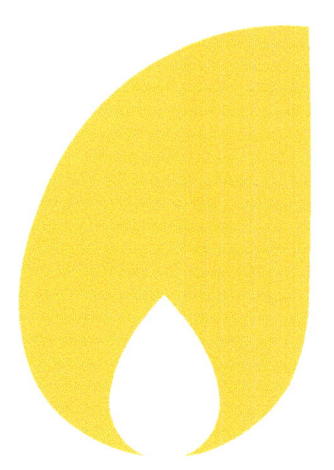

The Bible describes this journey in detail in Philippians 2:1-8. Use the SPECK method to study this passage.

45

SINS TO AVOID

Make a list of any sins—wrong actions, attitudes, or thoughts—mentioned in the passage. These are the things to avoid in your life.

PROMISES TO CLAIM

Make a list of the promises in this passage. Promises give us confidence when we doubt God or face difficult times. So take them to heart and believe what they say.

EXAMPLES TO FOLLOW

What examples do you find in the passage? Is there a right way of thinking or acting described in the passage that you should take as an example for your life? Write it down.

COMMANDS TO OBEY

Write out all the commands you find. If a passage encourages you to take a certain action, take it as a command and write it down.

KNOWLEDGE OF GOD TO APPLY

What does the passage tell you about God that you can apply to your daily life? God's character shines throughout the Bible as an example for us.

DAY SIX
INVISIBLE

There are invisible people in your world. I'm not talking about imaginary friends or paranormal activity. This isn't about the latest vampire movie or ghost hunter TV show. It's a lot scarier than that—because it's real.

You pass them in the hallways at school. You sit across from them on the bus. They live a few houses down the road. And you don't even notice them.

Okay, maybe you know their names. But based on the way you treat them, they might as well be invisible. One of the biggest ironies of service is that we're willing to travel to other countries thousands of miles away to care for people from other cultures, while we completely ignore people we see every single day.

Don't feel too bad—it happens to all of us. But that doesn't mean it's okay. Jesus has a special eye for the lost, the hurting, and the invisible. He often tossed aside his comfort and his popularity for opportunities to serve people the rest of the world didn't really see, like lepers, prostitutes, and sinners. One of the ways we can become more like Jesus is to start seeing the world through his eyes. Are you ready? Take the following challenge:

OPERATION INVISIBLE

In this challenge, your goal is to identify the "invisible" people in your world and figure out how to serve them. Follow these steps:

1. Pray.

God is an expert at seeing and caring for invisible people. Thankfully his Holy Spirit can teach you to see them as he does. Take a few minutes to ask God to give you eyes to see the people in your world you've ignored in the past. Invite him to bring to your mind any specific people he wants you to think about.

2. Watch.

For the next few days, keep a special eye out for "invisible" people in your world. Write down their names. This could be at school, at work, around town, or even at home. Write their names in the list on the next page.

1.	11.
2.	12.
3.	13.
4.	14.
5.	15.
6.	16.
7.	17.
8.	18.
9.	19.
10.	20.

3. Select.

If you've done your job well, after only a few days you'll have a long list. You probably can't serve all of these people regularly, so ask God to help you pick five people you could begin to serve, whether in big ways or small. (Don't forget your family!) Write their names in the chart below.

4. See.

The first step to making invisible people visible is to notice things about them. Maybe it's a routine they have, a thing they love, or the way they act around other people. Next to each name in the chart, write one important thing you've noticed about that person. Try to look beyond clothes, style, and other superficial things.

5. Sacrifice.

Think of one sacrifice you could make for each of these people. True service doesn't reward us—it demands something of us. You could sacrifice your time, your popularity, your comfort, or something else. Just remember not to turn these people into charity cases. Once you've finished filling in the chart, commit to actually making these sacrifices!

Name	What I See	What I Can Sacrifice

DAY SEVEN
ALWAYS VIGILANT

Remember a week ago when we talked about the Sabbath, the special day God set aside for us to rest? People in Jesus' time took the Sabbath very seriously. They looked down on anyone who did any work at all on that day of the week. But when we read about Jesus' ministry, we see him healing people and teaching on the Sabbath. The religious leaders didn't like this at all. They criticized Jesus for working on the day God gave people to rest.

But these leaders just didn't get it. Jesus told them that, even though rest and devotion to God are important, they're never an excuse to avoid helping people who need it. Disease, hunger, and pain don't take a break once a week. We should be ready to serve others in need, even at the end of a long day, on the weekend, and during a vacation. So go ahead and take the day off from journaling and doing challenges in this book! But if you see an opportunity to serve, go for it.

"HE SAID TO THEM, 'IF ANY OF YOU HAS A SHEEP AND IT FALLS INTO A PIT ON THE SABBATH, **will you not take hold of it** AND LIFT IT OUT? HOW MUCH MORE VALUABLE IS A PERSON THAN A SHEEP! THEREFORE IT IS LAWFUL TO DO GOOD ON THE SABBATH.'"

Matthew 12:11-12

Week Four
HOW DO WE SERVE?

DAY ONE
INTRO

Imagine waking up in a good mood. You slept as long as you needed to, you're excited about your plans for the day, and you smell a delicious breakfast cooking in the kitchen. Your mom asks, "How are you this morning?" You smile and answer, "I'm awesome!"

But suppose you woke up in a bad mood. You were up half the night because the neighbor's dog was barking, you have a test in your first class, and all you can smell are your dirty clothes piling up next to your bed. Your mom asks, "How are you this morning?" You frown and answer, "I'm *awesome*."

Anyone who's used sarcasm knows that how you say something is just as important as what you say. Tone, volume, and body language carry just as much of the message as the actual words. The same is true of what you do.

Maybe you've heard someone say something like, "The ends justify the means," or "To make an omelet, you have to break a few eggs." What they mean is, as long as the result is positive, the way they achieved that result doesn't matter. But most of us know that's not true. Why? Because *how* matters.

In God's eyes, the way we serve makes a huge difference. How? You'll find out this week.

AT ARM'S LENGTH

Serving others in love lifts us out of our comfort zones and introduces us to situations we wouldn't experience otherwise. It's both humbling and empowering. The best part? It's an adventure that brings us closer to the heart of Jesus.

John 3:16-17 says, "For God so loved the world that he gave his one and only Son, that whoever believes in him shall not perish but have eternal life. For God did not send his Son into the world to condemn the world, but to save the world through him." You see, Jesus could have tried to communicate his love for us from far away, staying at arm's length. But God knew that people needed Jesus to be near to them. They needed to witness his sacrificial love on the Cross. They needed to interact with Jesus—to touch him, to see his face, to hear his voice.

Think of your worst day ever. You're in your room, alone, depressed, and the world seems to be falling apart. Which do you want more in that situation: an encouraging text, a "get better soon" card, or a best friend with you in the same room?

Now think about how you serve? Do you pick and choose, using service to build your image? Or are you selfless and authentic, willing to get messy to meet needs where they are, not just from a distance?

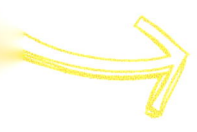

Who are you closest to at school? At home? At church?

Who do you try to avoid at school? At home? At church?

Where do you spend most of your time? Where do you avoid going if at all possible?

Who at school, home, and church needs your help the most? Why?

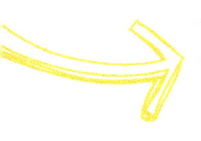

What barriers are keeping you from going where people need your help or getting close enough to help them?

DAY TWO
PRAYER

Have you ever told someone you would pray for them, only to completely forget about it five minutes later? We've all been there! But praying for someone, as easy as it may seem, can be an incredibly powerful form of service. We can show love to others by lifting them up to God in prayer. This can be a life-changing discipline for any Christ-follower.

Jesus prayed for his disciples. He interceded for them in prayer—and for you. You can find Jesus' prayer for his followers in John 17:6-26. Intercessory prayer is simply praying for, or "on behalf of" others, praising God for the ways he has blessed them, and asking God to provide for their needs. Intercessory prayer is a way for you to spend time with God and care for others at the same time. He hears you and cares for the people you're praying for even more than you do!

Ephesians 6:18 tells us to "pray in the Spirit on all occasions with all kinds of prayers and requests. With this in mind, be alert and always keep on praying for all the Lord's people." Praying for others isn't just a suggestion—it's something we should be doing all the time.

Prayer works for the good of the person you're praying for, but it also changes you. God uses our prayer lives to shape how we see people and to make us more attuned to the needs of those around us. Take the following challenge:

WEEK OF PRAYER

Think right now about the people in your life you see every day. Do you pray for them? Do you pray for friends who aren't Christ-followers? What about your brothers and sisters in Christ? Do you pray for your family? Do you ever pray for the people you don't like very much?

Write down one person from each of these groups: acquaintances, believing friends, non-believing friends, family members, enemies (or even frenemies). Your challenge is to pray for each of these people at least three times this week. Check off a box each time you pray for one of these people.

acquaintance ☐ ☐ ☐

believing friend ☐ ☐ ☐

non-believing friend ☐ ☐ ☐

family member ☐ ☐ ☐

enemy/frenemy ☐ ☐ ☐

DAY THREE
SERVE WITH WORDS

Yesterday, we looked at how we can serve people by talking to God. But there's someone else we can talk with to help others—the people we're serving! When we speak encouragement into someone's life, we do more good than we can possibly imagine.

Do you remember the last time someone pointed out a special talent you have or complimented something you did? Or perhaps they told you they really liked or respected you. That encouragement probably stuck with you for a long time afterward, pushing you to do bigger and greater things. Whether you know it or not, that kind of support is a very important part of our emotional health. Without it, we don't function well.

Kind and encouraging words are an important but neglected part of service. You might be surprised by how many people don't hear those words at home. People long for someone to speak truth into their lives—to recognize their achievements, to compliment them on their features, and to let them know that someone cares about them. A small word of appreciation can go a long way toward showing someone that they're valued.

What we say is just as important in service as what we do. Be an encourager. Build others up; don't tear others down. Don't worry about saying the exact "right" thing. Focus on saying good things. Ask God for the wisdom and courage to speak up. You never know how you could change someone's life with one simple word.

Read 1 Thessalonians 5:9-15, and then choose one of the Bible study methods out of the three you've been using over the last few weeks.

5P (page 8)
OPA (page 24)
SPECK (page 30)

DAY FOUR
SERVICE UNDERCOVER

We all know people who want the world to know how generous they are. They constantly share pictures of themselves serving in some way. On Twitter they post things like, "So thankful I have the opportunity to give to charity #blessed." They may be helping others, but somehow they always seem to make it about themselves.

In Jesus' time, people did the same thing. Religious leaders made sure others watched as they gave money to the poor. They wanted people to hear every single coin clink into the temple treasury as they emptied their pockets. But Jesus said,

> "when you give to the needy, do not announce it with trumpets, as the hypocrites do in the synagogues and on the streets, to be honored by men. … but when you give to the needy, do not let your left hand know what your right hand is doing, so that your giving may be in secret"
> (Matthew 6:2-4a).

Next time you serve someone, think about how you're doing it. Are you making it about yourself, bragging to anyone who will listen? Or are you genuinely worried about the person you are serving, unconcerned with whether or not anyone knows what you've done? Read this quote from Martin Luther King Jr. and answer the following questions.

"The first question that the priest asked, the first question that the Levite asked was, 'If I stop to help this man, what will happen to me?' But then the Good Samaritan came by, and he reversed the question: 'If I do not stop to help this man, what will happen to him?'" -Martin Luther King Jr., "I've Been to the Mountaintop" speech

According to Martin Luther King Jr., how are the priest and the Levite different from the Good Samaritan?

Think back to the last time you were praised for doing an act of service. Would the experience have been different if no one knew about it? If so, how?

What is something you could do today to serve another person without them finding out?

**Disciples of Christ serve SELFLESSLY.
(Mark 12:41-43)**

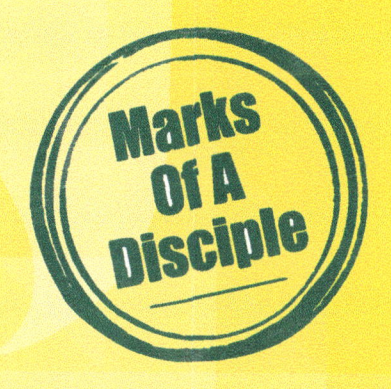

Marks Of A Disciple

DAY FIVE
HERE, THERE, EVERYWHERE

Service opportunities are closer than we realize. While they are certainly in other countries and cities, they are also in your own city and home. Did you know that Jesus probably never traveled much farther than 100 miles from his hometown during his ministry? And the bulk of his work was done in a much smaller area than that! His service and ministry were in the surrounding towns, with people who were right there in his community—and yet, his service was so effective that its ripple effects have created believers on every continent throughout the world.

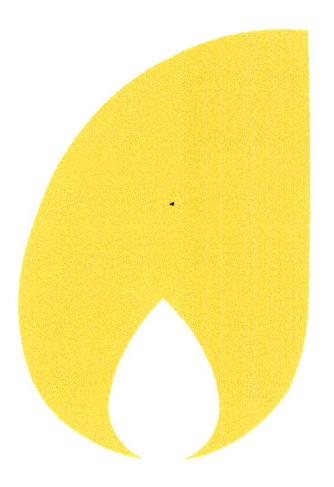

There is no service too small or too great for us if we do it out of Christ's love. God uses each of us to reach and serve the lost and needy close to us and in other countries around the globe. It's not about what we can do—it's about what God can do through us.

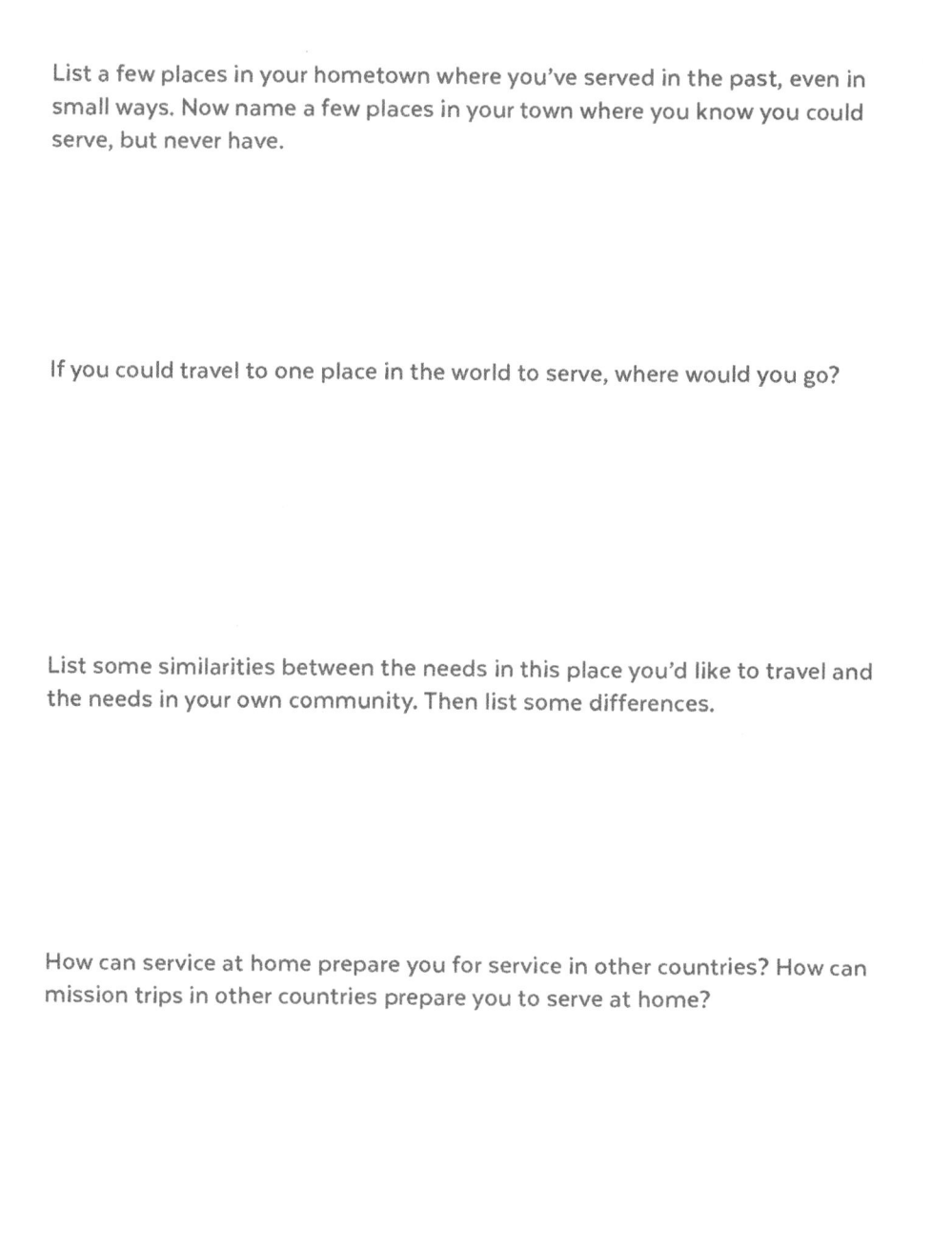

List a few places in your hometown where you've served in the past, even in small ways. Now name a few places in your town where you know you could serve, but never have.

If you could travel to one place in the world to serve, where would you go?

List some similarities between the needs in this place you'd like to travel and the needs in your own community. Then list some differences.

How can service at home prepare you for service in other countries? How can mission trips in other countries prepare you to serve at home?

DAY SIX
INTO THE WORLD

Sometimes serving is a blast. If you've ever been on a mission trip, I'm sure you have some pretty great memories and some legendary stories. Serving can take you places you never thought you'd go, where you meet people you never imagined meeting and you do things you never dreamed of doing. Serving can take us to the mountaintops of our relationship with Christ and can give us a summit view of his kingdom.

But you've probably noticed that a lot of this journal has focused on the hard parts of service, the parts that half-hearted and uncommitted people avoid. That's because what makes someone a servant isn't a particular type of service. It's the willingness to serve at any time, in any place, for anyone. The evidence of servanthood can be found in our ability to serve in the not-so-great and not-so-convenient times.

Thankfully we can look to Jesus, the ultimate servant, for encouragement and motivation. Serving is about putting ourselves last and others first. It's about looking for ways to meet the needs of those who can't meet their own. And it's about loving the world the way Christ loves the world.

During his earthly ministry, Jesus said that it's better to give than to receive (Acts 20:35). He was partially talking about the heavenly rewards we'll receive for serving as a Christ-follower, but he was also talking about the ways in which serving can deeply bless us here and now. Service connects you to Jesus in a way you'd never be able to otherwise!

What are a few things you have learned over the last four weeks?

Do you still have questions about service? Who could you speak to about those questions?

What holds you back from serving in the unexpected ways you learned about over the last few weeks?

What excites you about living a life of service?

What are some practical ways to constantly remind yourself to live every day as a servant?

DAY SEVEN
WRAPPING UP

You know the drill by now. Today is your day off! It's also the last day of this entire study.

Congratulations!

While you may not have any more questions to answer or challenges to complete, your adventure of becoming a servant is just beginning. You should notice by now that every week had a rhythm to it. You studied what the Bible taught about helping others, discovered what some wise people had to say about service, looked closely at the role of service in your own life, took challenges to stretch yourself, and rested by spending time with God. None of these things have to stop just because you're done with this book.

You've heard it over and over, but here it is again: service is an all-the-time thing. It's a fundamental part of our relationships with Jesus. So follow his lead. Love the people he loves. See them the way he sees them. And serve them in big and small ways every chance you get.

It's more than just a nice thing to do; it's who you are.

You are a servant!

NOTES:: Quotations taken from THE COMPLETE GATHERED GOLD, A treasury of quotations for Christians. John Blanchard, ed. Evangelical Press, 2006.

deep
DISCIPLESHIP

A ONE-YEAR, COMPREHENSIVE STRATEGY FOR GROWING DISCIPLES

www.deepdiscipleship.com

Powered By: LeaderTreks

LeaderTreks®

PARTNERING WITH YOUTH WORKERS TO DEVELOP STUDENT LEADERS

RESOURCES | TRAINING | COACHING | TRIPS

877.502.0699
leadertreks.com